CRAFT TOPICS

TUDORS

FACTS • THINGS TO MAKE • ACTIVITIES

RACHEL WRIGHT

Watts Books

dney

& York

© 1993 Watts Books

Paperback edition 1994
This edition 1995

Watts Books
96 Leonard Street
London EC2A 4RH

Franklin Watts
14 Mars Road
Lane Cove
NSW 2006

UK ISBN: 0 7496 1138 3 (hardback)
         0 7496 1798 5 (paperback)

10 9 8 7 6 5 4 3 2 1

Editor: Hazel Poole
Designed: Sally Boothroyd
Consultant: Dr. A Hassell Smith, Rosemary Harden
Photography by: Chris Fairclough
Artwork by: Ed Dovey

A CIP catalogue record for this book
is available from the British Library

Printed in the United Kingdom

CONTENTS

From 1485 to 1603, England was ruled by a royal family called the Tudors. As you read this book and meet the family one by one, you might find it helpful to turn back to this page and remind yourself how they were all related.

TUDOR COAT OF ARMS

Henry VII m. **Elizabeth of York**
1485-1509   (d.1503)

Arthur m. **Catherine of Aragon**
(d.1502)

Henry VIII m. 1. **Catherine of Aragon**
1509-1547   (div. 1533)

2. **Anne Boleyn**
(ex. 1536)

3. **Jane Seymour**
(d. 1537)

4. **Anne of Cleves**
(div. 1540)

5. **Catherine Howard**
(ex. 1542)

6. **Catherine Parr**
(d. 1548)

Margaret m. **James IV of Scotland**
(d.1541)   1488-1513

James V of Scotland
1513-1542

Mary I m. **Philip II of Spain**
1553-1558   (d. 1598)

Elizabeth I
1558-1603

Edward VI
1547-1553

Mary, Queen of Scots
1542-1567
(ex. 1587)
m. 1. **Francis II of France** (d.1560)
2. **Henry, Lord Darnley** (d.1567)

James VI of Scotland
1567-1625
(**James I of England**)
1603-1625

👑	= reigned
m.	= married
div.	= divorced
d.	= died
ex.	= executed

4

HENRY AND SON

The age of the Tudors began on the 22 August 1485, when a Welsh nobleman by the name of Henry Tudor defeated King Richard III at the Battle of Bosworth. The story goes that just before Richard died, the English crown fell off his head and into a bush. Quick as a flash, one of Henry's men spotted it, placed it on his leader's head, and crowned him Henry VII, King of England.

Henry's victory proved to be a turning point in English history. For many years, two noble families – the Lancasters and the Yorks – had squabbled and schemed about which of them should rule England. Henry, who was part Lancastrian himself, put an end to the feuding by marrying Elizabeth of York, the daughter of King Edward IV. In so doing, he united the Yorks and Lancasters into a new royal family – the Tudors.

TAMING THE NOBILITY

As soon as he was married, Henry set about controlling the power of his overmighty nobles. He banned their private armies and made sure that they were punished if they broke the law. These measures helped to restore order to the country, which for too long had been ravaged and ruled by a warring nobility.

MAKING MONEY

Henry was a great businessman. He kept a close watch on all the Crown's finances, and taxed and fined his subjects whenever he could. Although he ruled with the help of a few personally selected ministers, the success of his peaceful money-raising policies was largely due to his own good business sense. When he died in 1509, he left the royal money chests well filled.

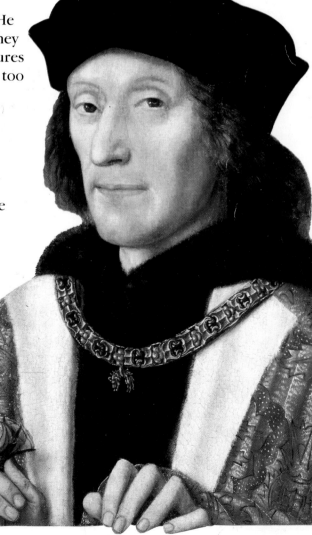

▶ *Henry VII*

▼ *The Tudor Rose was the emblem of Henry VII and his family. By uniting the white rose of York and the red rose of Lancaster it showed that the two families were now joined together in a new dynasty.*

THE KING'S CHANCELLOR

When Henry VII's son, Henry VIII, first came to the throne in 1509, he left the business of government to his Chancellor, Thomas Wolsey. Proud and powerful, Wolsey handled England's affairs well. Yet he fell from favour in 1529, when he failed to secure a divorce for his king.

▶ Cardinal Wolsey

▲ Henry VIII

A QUESTION OF DIVORCE

Henry was desperate to divorce his Spanish wife, Catherine of Aragon, and marry Anne Boleyn, whom he hoped would give him a son and heir. However, as England was a Catholic country, Henry knew that only the Pope, as head of the Catholic Church, had the right to grant him a divorce. So he sent Wolsey off to Rome to persuade the Pope to do just that.

Wolsey's request put the Pope in a very tricky position. He didn't want to upset Henry, but at the same time he didn't want to anger Catherine's nephew, Charles V of Spain, who opposed the divorce. So he sat back and did nothing. This enraged Henry, but it didn't stop him. In 1533, he divorced Catherine anyway and married Anne. He then broke off all relations with the Pope and the Catholic Church, and declared himself head of the Church of England.

MORE'S MURDER

Many were shocked by Henry's actions, including Wolsey's successor, Sir Thomas More. In 1532 he resigned his office, and three years later he was beheaded for refusing to accept Henry as head of the English Church.

THE END OF THE MONASTERIES

More's successor, Thomas Cromwell, is probably best known as the man who closed England's monasteries.

Henry wanted Cromwell to strip the monasteries of their land and wealth because he was bankrupt. His extravagant lifestyle and wars with France had emptied the royal purse, and he needed money to buy the support of his nobles, to stop them from siding with the Pope. Also, because the monasteries were loyal to the Pope, Henry saw them as a threat . . . and he wanted that threat removed!

Cromwell did not disappoint his king. By 1539, all the monasteries had been shut down and all their treasures had been confiscated.

Amongst his many achievements, Cromwell also succeeded in bringing Wales and the north of England under Tudor rule.

PROTESTANT PROGRESS

The destruction of the monasteries met with little resistance. For some time, the English had been dissatisfied with their monks, bishops and priests, many of whom they felt were greedy and sinful.

This growing mistrust of the Catholic clergy was not confined to England either. During the 1520s and 30s a new Christian religion, called Protestantism, had started to emerge in Europe. Its followers rejected the Pope's power, challenged many Catholic beliefs, and urged individuals to study the Bible for themselves.

Before Protestantism arrived on the scene, the Bible had always been written in Latin and studied by the clergy. In 1535, however, the first English translation of the Bible appeared, and two years later Henry allowed an English Bible to be used in his churches. England's conversion to Protestantism had begun.

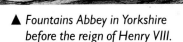

▲ Fountains Abbey in Yorkshire before the reign of Henry VIII.

▼ After Henry VIII closed the monasteries, Fountains Abbey was left to crumble away.

BLACK LETTERING

Like many important documents in the 1500s, The Great English Bible was written in Black lettering.

If you want to try writing in a similar style. . .

You will need: 2 x A4 sheets of white paper • 2 paper clips • a ruler • a broad-nibbed pen (a cartridge pen or a fibre-tipped calligraphy pen would be ideal).

Before you begin lettering, it's a good idea to draw some guide-lines, to help keep your letters straight.

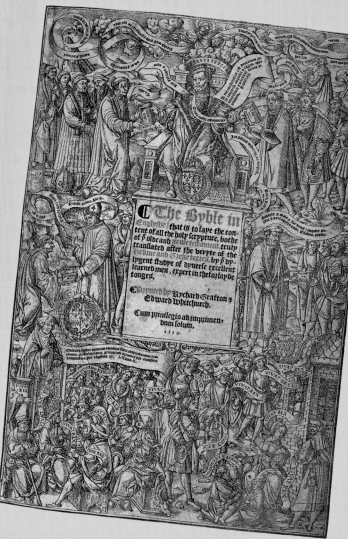

▲ The title page of the Great English Bible of 1539. At the top of the picture, Henry VIII is giving Bibles to his main advisers.

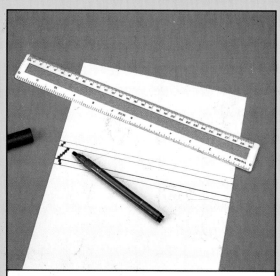

▲ **1.** Draw a heavy line across one of the sheets of paper, and then draw a fainter line above it. These two lines should be five nib-widths apart. Now draw two more lines. The first should be two nib-widths above the faint line, and the second should be two nib-widths below the heavy line.

2. Place a piece of paper over your guidesheet and attach it with the paper clips. Hold your pen so that its nib is at an angle of 45° to the guide-lines, and start practising different strokes. It's worth practising the 'I' shape quite a lot because it forms the basis of so many letters.

▶ (These letters have been written directly onto the guidesheet to show you how they should fit within the lines).

▼ **3.** When you've finished practising different lines and curves, try writing the whole alphabet. Remember to always keep your pen at an angle of 45°. Don't worry if your letters look a bit wobbly at first. Keep practising and they'll soon improve.

Although Catherine of Aragon had given birth to a daughter called Mary, Henry was not impressed. Like most people, he wanted a male heir to rule England after he died. So when Anne Boleyn also gave birth to a girl, Elizabeth, in 1533, Henry was furious. As a result he quickly lost interest in his wife, and in 1536 he had her beheaded!

With Anne gone, Henry was free to marry his latest love, Jane Seymour, and in 1537 she gave birth to a son – much to everyone's relief!

▲ Henry VIII, Jane Seymour and their son Edward

THE CHILD KING

When Henry VIII died in 1547, his nine year old son became King Edward VI. While the young king got on with his schoolwork, his advisers worked hard to further the Protestant cause. Amongst other things, they declared the Catholic Mass illegal, and introduced a new prayer book, which changed church services from Latin to English.

THE CATHOLIC QUEEN

Edward's reforms, however, were shortlived. In 1553 he fell ill and died and his Catholic half-sister, Mary, became queen. Once crowned, Mary began reversing her brother's anti-Catholic laws. She restored the Pope as Head of the English Church and persecuted those who opposed her policies.

In 1554 she made matters worse by marrying a Catholic, Philip II of Spain. The marriage caused a huge outcry in England, and when Mary died just four years later, few mourned her death.

◀ Mary I was nicknamed "bloody Mary" because she burned many Protestants at the stake.

ENTER ELIZABETH

England's next monarch, Elizabeth I, was a lot more tolerant than her sister. Although she had little sympathy for Catholics or extremist Protestants, she persecuted neither. Instead, she allowed certain Catholic rituals, but rejected the Pope's authority and encouraged church services in English. This policy seems to have suited most people, and those who disagreed with it were simply fined for not attending church regularly.

MINISTERS OF STATE

Much of the success of Elizabeth's moderate religious policy was due to her Archbishop of Canterbury, Matthew Parker. He was one of a group of ministers picked by the Queen to help her govern. Another was William Cecil, who was Elizabeth's chief adviser for 40 years. During that time he controlled England's finances, and helped to keep the Country from becoming too actively involved in the religious wars that were devastating Europe.

▼ Elizabeth I

▲ William Cecil

11

PLOTS AND DISCOVERIES

THE ROYAL CAPTIVE

Despite strong pressure from her parliament to marry, Elizabeth I remained single. This meant that for much of her reign, her Catholic cousin, Mary Stuart, Queen of Scots, was heir to the English throne. Mary's faith made her a potential enemy, so when she fled to England in 1568, having been deposed by her Protestant subjects, Elizabeth had no choice but to imprison her. This, however, proved to be a bad move on Elizabeth's part, because Mary immediately became the focus for a chain of Catholic intrigues – some of which were backed by Spain.

TROUBLE WITH SPAIN

During the 1560s, England and Spain had begun an unofficial war at sea. The cause of the conflict was Spain's refusal to let anyone trade with her wealthy colonies in Central and Southern America. This prompted English sailors to seek revenge by attacking Spanish colonies and treasure ships. Officially, the Queen had nothing to do with these piratical practices but, unofficially, she often took a share of the loot!

In 1585, the relationship between the two nations worsened when Elizabeth sent an army to the Netherlands to help Dutch Protestants get rid of their Spanish rulers. This infuriated Philip II of Spain, who rapidly set about backing plots to get rid of Elizabeth and enthrone Mary. Although none of these plots were successful, they hardened English opinion against Mary, and on 8 February 1587, she was beheaded.

THE COMING OF THE ARMADA

Mary's murder was the final blow as far as Philip was concerned, and in 1588, he sent a mighty fleet of ships, known as the Armada, to conquer England. This great invasion was not a success, though.

During the decade before the Armada, Sir John Hawkins had re-designed England's navy. Instead of the high, heavy galleons still used by Spain, he had built smaller, faster ships which were easy to handle and carried many guns. Aboard such ships, the English were able to cripple much of the Armada easily. The rest of the Spanish fleet was either burnt by fireships or damaged by storms on the way home.

ADVENTURES ON THE HIGH SEAS

The Elizabethan era was a time of daring discovery when many explorers sailed the world in search of distant shores and new trade routes. In 1577 Sir Francis Drake began his epic three year voyage around the world. In 1579 Sir Humphrey Gilbert set out to establish the first English colony in America, and in 1585 Sir Walter Raleigh tried to colonise Virginia.

Encouraged by England's improving seamanship, merchants set up new trading companies in London to push trade into Russia, Turkey and other far off lands. The success of these ventures helped to make London one of the richest cities in Europe.

▲ A model of the Golden Hind. *Captained by Sir Francis Drake, the* Golden Hind *was the first English ship to sail around the world.*

◄ *Painted shortly after the defeat of the Armada, this picture shows the English and Spanish fleets in battle.*

FRILLS AND FINERY

Elizabeth I loved jewel-encrusted clothes, and when she died in 1603, she is said to have left over 2,000 decorated dresses hanging in her wardrobe. Her courtiers dressed extravagantly too, in clothes made of velvet, silk and satin.

Most ordinary people wore clothes similar in line to those of the very fashionable, but their outfits were simpler, and made from cheaper materials, such as wool and linen.

Children, who were treated as miniature adults, were usually dressed in smaller versions of their parents' clothes. Look at the illustrations below and imagine what it would be like if you had to wear similar fashions today.

Corsets, known as "a pair of bodies" were stiffened with bundles of rushes or whalebone.

Petticoats, called farthingales, were stiffened with circular hoops of twisted fabric, rushes, whalebone or wire. These hoops must have made sitting down a nightmare!

Doublets were usually made of silk and velvet and were often decorated with embroidery or cuts in the fabric, known as slashing.

Boys sometimes wore unpadded jerkins over their doublets as well.

Canions

Girls wore silk or woollen hand-knitted stockings under their farthingales.

Dress sleeves were often attached by strings under the arms

The bodice and skirt of a dress were often separate and made from costly fabrics such as woven silk or embroidered velvet.

Breeches and doublets were padded with materials such as wool, horsehair, cotton and bran!

Ribbon-fastened stockings

Fashionable men prized their cloaks which could be worn in a variety of ways.

RUFF TIMES

As if the problems of farthingales and bran-stuffed trousers weren't enough, the Elizabethans also liked to wear starched linen collars called ruffs. These rigid neck rings started out fairly small but, as time went by they grew so ridiculously huge that wearers had to use special long-handled spoons to get their food into their mouths!

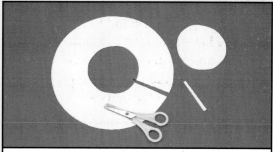

TO MAKE YOUR OWN REGULAR-SIZED RUFF

1. Draw around the dinner plate twice, and cut out the circles.

2. Measure around your neck and add 2 cms to this measurement. Then cut out a strip of card and draw a line on it, one sixth of the length of your neck measurement.

▲**4.** Cut both large circles as shown, and remove their centres.

5. Cut out a long strip of card, the same width as one of your card rings. Pleat the strip so that it forms a zig-zag. Glue this pleated strip onto one of the rings. Put the other ring around your neck and place the pleated ring on top of it.

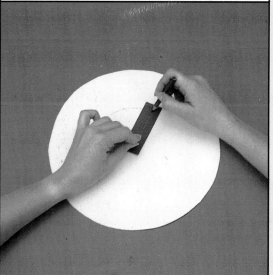

▲**3.** Push the pin first through one end of this line and then into the centre of one of the circles. Push the tip of your pencil through the other end of the line and, holding the pin firmly, swing the pencil round to draw a circle. Repeat this with the other card circle.

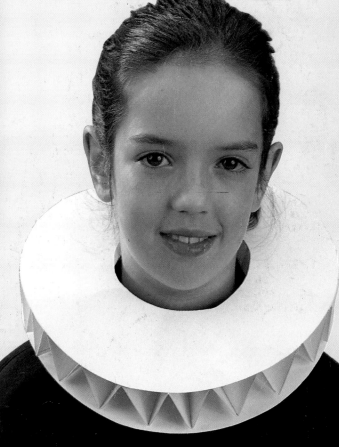

COUNTRY LIVING

In Tudor times, most people lived in the country and farmed the land. Wheat, oats, barley, corn and rye were the main crops grown and everything, from sowing to harvesting, was done by hand, with the aid of simple tools.

SOCIAL STRUCTURES

Country life was ruled by the gentry. Like the nobility above them, the gentry were well-born and often owned several thousand acres of land. They also had great influence in their own counties, which they governed on behalf of the Crown.

Next in line to the gentry were the towns' merchants and then the yeomanry. The yeomanry was mostly made up of large-scale farmers who sometimes cultivated 200-300 acres.

Below the merchants and yeomen came the craftsmen and small-scale farmers. The fortunes of these two groups varied, and sometimes they were forced to join the unemployed who, like the general labourers, enjoyed few privileges.

PROFIT AND POVERTY

At the start of the Tudor period, England and Wales were underpopulated. This was because a deadly disease called the Black Death had swept through Europe in the 1300s and killed millions of people. Both countries were also underdeveloped, with most villages growing just about enough food to feed themselves.

After about 1525, however, the population began to grow rapidly. This caused the price of food and goods to soar. In order to keep pace with these rising prices, landlords had to make their property as profitable as possible. So they kept wages low, joined small farms together to make more productive ones, and cleared wasteland and forests for agricultural use. They also took over

common land, where small-scale farmers were allowed to graze their cattle, and used it to rear their own sheep. All this caused great distress amongst the smaller farmers and labourers, many of whom became beggars.

ELIZABETHAN ENTERPRISE

Rising prices and an increased demand for goods not only stimulated farmers to sell their crops for a profit. They also encouraged the development of lots of industries, including coal, tin, lead, copper and iron ore mining.

To make iron from ore, manufacturers needed to burn vast amounts of wood in their furnaces. England's thriving dockyards also needed lots of wood to build ships. This growing demand for timber soon threatened to drain the country's forests. As a result, coal began to replace wood as the fuel most used for cooking and heating.

▼ *Sheep farming was a profitable business in Tudor times because wool was England's most valuable export. Using common land for sheep pasture was unpopular though, because it meant employment for just one shepherd and no-one else.*

TUDOR HOMES

COUNTRY HOUSES

As the Tudor Age became more peaceful and prosperous, the houses of the nobility and gentry became more comfortable. Unlike the castle homes of medieval nobles which were built for defence, Elizabethan nobles built themselves magnificent mansions with wide glass windows, decorated chambers, open courtyards and huge, formal gardens.

The interiors of these new mansions also offered more privacy than those of castle times. Instead of having to sleep and entertain in the same room, some wealthy families now had separate bedrooms and parlours. Many of the larger mansions also had long, window-lined galleries where people could dance and walk on wet days.

TIMBER HOMES AND MUD HUTS

Many Elizabethan mansions were built of stone or brick, but most other houses, both grand and small, were timber-framed, with wattle and daub, or clay and rubble walls.

By the end of Elizabeth's reign many prosperous merchants and yeoman were living in timber-framed houses with six rooms or more. Poorer people, however, often had to make do with much less space. Some families had only one room in a town house. Others lived in single roomed cottages or small, dingy huts made from mud, straw and lime.

▲ Hardwick Hall in Derbyshire was built for Elizabeth, Countess of Shrewsbury in the 1590s.

▼ In Tudor times, lots of people started to put brick chimneystacks into their homes. Those without fireplaces or chimneys had a fire in the middle of their main room, and openings in the roof to let out the smoke.

FURNITURE

Although the homes of the wealthy were far better furnished than those of the poor, they were still uncomfortable by our standards. Rich households had carved wooden chests, stools, cupboards, tables and a few chairs, but they didn't have electric lights, running water or toilets. Instead they had to sew by candle-light, wash in bowls filled with water from jugs, and go to the toilet in a chamber pot or in an outside hut placed over a hole in the ground.

The most prized pieces of furniture in many of these homes were the four poster beds, which were passed down from one generation to the next. Rich yeomen and their families had low beds on castors, which could be stored under higher beds, but most poor people just slept on a straw mattress on the floor.

▲ Town houses were often built upwards instead of outwards, to save space. Some had as many as five storeys, each one jutting out over the one below. Houses like this were often built on both sides of a narrow cobbled street. This made the street below gloomy and smelly, because the buildings blocked out the light and trapped the smell of the rubbish that littered every street.

19

Card is easier to fold if it has been scored first. To score a straight line, gently run the tip of your scissors along the line, using a ruler to guide you.

You will need: a cereal packet (the largest you can find) • glue • scissors • ruler • paper • poster paints • pencil • thin card • a cocktail stick.

TO MAKE THE ROOFS

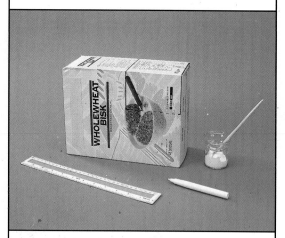

▲ **1.** Glue the opening to your cereal packet shut and mark the box, as shown.

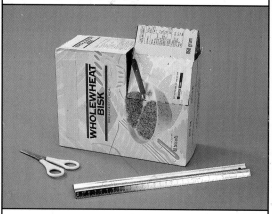

▲ **2.** Score the dotted lines, cut through the solid ones and fold the centre line to form a roof.

3. Glue the side of the box to the roof and trim the edges.

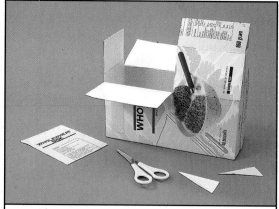

▲ **4.** Cut away the rest of the top of the box, as shown, and open out the sides.

▲ **5.** Glue the piece of card you have just removed from the top of the box onto the open side of the roof. Then trim one of the opened out flaps so that it is slightly shorter than the other. Fold the top of the longer flap into a tab and glue the two flaps together to form a second roof.

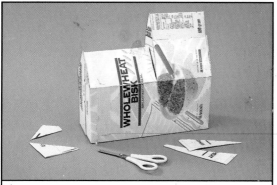

▲6. Glue the gaping end of the second roof together and trim all the roof's edges, as shown. Use the spare bits of card to cover the gap at the top of the first roof.

TO MAKE THE ROOF TILES

▲9. Cut and paint several strips of card as shown, and glue them onto your roofs. Now paint the rest of your house.

TO MAKE THE GROUND FLOOR

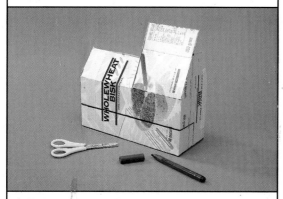

▲7. Mark the box as shown and cut along these lines.

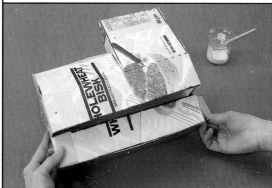

▲8. Open out the lower part of the house and glue it under the upper part.

TO MAKE A CHIMNEY

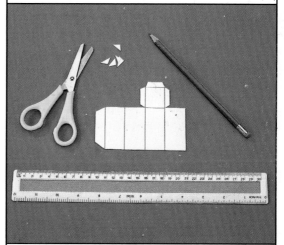

▲10. Divide a strip of card into four equal-sized panels with a tab at one end. Add a square with tabs, as shown, and cut the whole shape out.

▲ **11.** Glue all the tabs down to make a chimney. Now hold the chimney against the edge of the roof and mark it where it meets the roof. Cut along this line and then cut straight across the front and back of the chimney. Finally, cut the remaining side so that it matches the first side.

12. To make a chimney pot, cover one side of a thin strip of paper with glue and roll it around a cocktail stick. When you've made as many pots as you need, glue them into place. Then decorate your chimney and stick it into position.

▲ *Moreton Old Hall in Cheshire — a timber-framed gentry house.*

ROGUES AND BEGGARS

Throughout the Tudor period bands of vagabonds roamed the country, begging and stealing. Some of these beggars were too old or crippled to work. Others were able-bodied men and women who had lost their jobs and homes.

At first, beggars had to rely on charity to keep them from death's door. But, during Elizabeth's reign, laws were passed which said that every parish had to look after its own poor. Under these new laws, richer people had to contribute to the upkeep of the poor according to the amount of land they farmed.

CRIME AND PUNISHMENT

Not all beggars were genuine down-and-outs, though. Some were crafty conmen who ate soap to make themselves foam at the mouth so that passers-by would think they were sick and give them money.

Like the pickpockets who haunted the dark town streets, conmen were punished harshly if they were caught. Lazy beggars who refused to work were whipped until they bled, and small-time crooks were put into the stocks and pelted with rotting food. Highway robbers, thieves and murderers were sometimes hanged in public.

Tudor England didn't have a police force. Men took it in turns to act as a constable, and keep an eye on their village or town.

PLAYS AND PASTIMES

Plays were very popular in Tudor times and people from all levels of society went to see them. At first these plays were simply acted on carts in the streets. Later on, however, they were put on in the courtyards of inns and, during the late 1500s, they were staged in London's first theatres.

These early open-air theatres were informal, rowdy places. Keen to see the latest action-packed drama by William Shakespeare or Christopher Marlowe, the wealthy sat in covered galleries which ran around the theatre's walls, while poor play-goers crowded in front of the stage.

▲ Most plays were put on in the afternoon because theatres relied on the sun to light the stage.

FUN FIGHTS

As well as going to the theatre, everybody enjoyed playing bowls, cards, dice and board games, and singing and dancing to the accompaniment of live music. Cock fights and bear baiting were popular pastimes, too.

As the nobility and gentry had more leisure time and money than most, they also spent hours deer hunting, hawking and fencing. They occasionally jousted as well. Jousts were contests between armoured men on horseback. Armed with a lance, each rider had to charge towards his opponent and try to knock him off his horse.

Ordinary people also liked to play outdoor games, particularly football. But, with no referee and an unlimited number of players on each side, Tudor football matches were more like organized riots than sport.

▼ Henry VIII jousting in front of his first wife, Catherine of Aragon.

SCHOOLDAYS

Although there were infant schools in Tudor England, many poor children did not attend because they had to help their parents at home. Those who did go to these village schools, however, were often only half-taught to read by a priest or a poor woman in need of a job.

The sons, and sometimes the daughters, of the nobility and gentry were much better catered for. They were taught to read and write at home by private tutors.

▼ Boys had to learn most of their lessons by heart because books were scarce and paper was too expensive to use regularly.

OFF TO GRAMMAR SCHOOL

At the age of seven, wealthy boys often left their village class or private tutor and went to grammar school. Those who still couldn't sign their own name had to go to a petty school first, where they were taught to read and write.

Life at a Tudor grammar school must have been grim. The holidays were short, the school days were long, and anyone who misbehaved was beaten with a wooden rod.

The subjects taught weren't particularly varied, either. The main ones were Latin, Greek, public speaking (rhetoric), religion, arithmetic, geometry and astronomy. A lot of emphasis was placed on learning Latin because it was an international language. Even when they chatted amongst themselves, pupils were expected to use it instead of English.

AFTER-SCHOOL

When they left grammar school at about 16, boys who could afford it went on to Oxford or Cambridge University. The subjects that they studied there were similar to those taught at grammar school, only the lessons were a lot harder!

Would-be lawyers, and those who needed legal knowledge to run their estates, left school at about 14 and went to one of the Inns of Court instead. There they studied law and French, which was the language of the Courts.

Not all boys completed a formal education, though. On leaving school many went to live and work with a master craftsman, so that they could learn the skills of his trade.

▶ Early reading books were called horn books because the sheet of paper with the alphabet on it was protected by a see-through layer of animal horn. Each book was often hung from a pupil's belt by its wooden handle.

EDUCATING GIRLS

Girls rarely went to school. Instead they usually stayed at home and learnt how to be good wives and mothers.

By the end of the 1500s, however, there were a number of boarding schools for the daughters of the rich, but they weren't very scholarly. As one young lady complained, all the pupils were ever taught to do was to "frisk and dance, to paint their faces [and] to curl their hair".

Marzipan Matters

Sugar was very expensive in Tudor times, but those who could afford to, ate it in huge quantities. Custards, crystallized fruits and marchpanes (marzipan sweets) were all very popular, as was a toothpowder made from sugar, honey, fruit peel and crushed bones. No wonder Tudor portraits never show anyone smiling!

TO MAKE YOUR OWN MODERN DAY MARCHPANE . . .

Ask an adult to help you when you use the knife.

You will need: 125g ground almonds • 225g icing sugar • 1 egg • food colouring paste • a mixing bowl • a small bowl • a mug • sieve • wooden spoon • sharp knife • wooden rolling pin • wooden board • palette knife • cocktail stick • a lemon.

1. Sift the icing sugar into the mixing bowl and stir in the almonds.

2. Crack the egg on the side of the small bowl and carefully pull the shell apart. Holding the egg over the bowl, gently tip the yolk between the two shells until all the egg white has run into the bowl. Drop the yolk into the mug and put it to one side.

3. Beat the egg white lightly with the fork and add it to the almond and sugar mixture. Blend everything together, first with the spoon and then with your hands, until you have a smooth, firm paste.
   If your paste seems crumbly, add a little lemon juice to make it soft but not wet.

4 If you want to make marzipan sweets in the shape of a Tudor Rose, divide your paste into two portions. Put a small amount of red paste colour in the centre of one of them and knead it until the colour is evenly distributed.

▲5. Dust your rolling pin and board with icing sugar. Roll out both portions of marzipan until they are quite thin, and then cut as many petal shapes as you want. Use a cocktail stick to curl the top edge of each petal slightly.

6. Lift the petals off the board with the palette knife and arrange them so that they just overlap. Leave your roses to chill in the fridge for about 30 minutes, and then put on your ruff and tuck in!

THE SCOTTISH CONNECTION

Ever since King Edward I of England had tried to overrun Scotland in the late 1200s, there had been persistent hostility between the two kingdoms. Raiders from each side regularly crossed the border, and every truce ever declared was quickly broken.

When the Scots later backed a failed attempt to overthrow Henry VII, he decided that it was time to end this ancient hatred once and for all. He therefore proposed that his young daughter Margaret should marry King James IV of Scotland. After a number of delays, James finally agreed to the union, and in 1502 the couple were married.

The marriage did not settle the difficulties between the two countries straight away, though. Henry VIII went to war with Scotland twice during his reign and Edward VI, once during his.

Yet despite all this battle and bloodshed, the marriage did eventually serve its purpose. In 1566 the couple's grandaughter, Mary Stuart, Queen of Scots, gave birth to a son, who became James VI of Scotland. When Elizabeth I died in 1603, James inherited her throne and became the ruler of both lands.

▲ *James I of England (James VI of Scotland).*

Relations between the two kingdoms had greatly improved under Elizabeth, because she had helped Scottish Protestants achieve supremacy at home. By uniting the two Crowns, James helped to seal this new found bond, and it was on this optimistic note that the age of the Stuarts began.

▼ *Funeral procession of Elizabeth I.*

GLOSSARY

Astronomy – the study of stars, planets, comets, etc.

Bear-baiting – a cruel sport which involved chaining a bear to a post so that it could be teased and attacked by dogs.

Chamber pot – a pot which was kept in the bedroom and used as a toilet.

Chancellor – a chief minister.

Dynasty – a line of kings and queens from the same family.

Fence, to – to attack and defend with a sword.

Fireship – a ship which was stuffed full of things that would burn easily. It was then set alight and sent towards an enemy fleet. In 1588, whilst the Spanish Armada was anchored off France, the English sent in six fireships. To escape these burning ships, the Spanish scattered into the Channel, where they were heavily battered by English guns.

Geometry – a type of mathematics.

Hawk, to – to hunt with trained hawks. Hawks are birds of the falcon family.

Iron ore – a solid mineral from which iron is made.

Labourer – a man who did farm work for whoever would employ him.

Lance – a long, tapering wooden pole used for jousting.

Legal – anything related to law.

Mass – a Roman Catholic church service.

Medieval – of the Middle Ages. The Middle Ages is the name given to the period of history from about the 700s to 1500 A.D.

Monarch – a king or queen.

Monastery – a religious house for monks or nuns.

Parish – an area served by a church.

Parlour – a private sitting-room. Originally parlours were rooms in monasteries in which visitors could talk to the monks. When the monasteries were destroyed, the word was used to describe intimate sitting- or dining-rooms in private houses.

Seamanship – the art of handling ships at sea.

Vagabond – a wanderer, with no permanent home.

Wattle and daub – woven twigs filled in with mud and dung and used as a building material.

PLACES TO VISIT

Britain has lots of Tudor houses and museums, some of which are listed here. If you want further information about houses and museums in your area, contact your local tourist board.

STATELY HOMES

Little Morton Hall,
Congleton, Cheshire, CW12 4SD
Tel: 0260 272018
A fine timber-framed moated manor house.

Hardwick Hall,
Doe Lea, Chesterfield, S44 5QJ
Tel: 0246 850430.
This late 16th century mansion contains a
lot of Tudor furniture and needlework.

Hampton Court Palace,
Hampton Court, East Mosely,
Surrey, KT8 9AU
Tel: 081-977 8441
This royal palace was built by Wolsey in
1514, and given to Henry VIII in 1525 in an
attempt to regain royal favour. Rumour has it
that the palace is haunted by Jane Seymour
and Henry's fifth wife, Catherine Howard.

Hatfield House,
Hatfield, Herts
Tel: 0707 262823

Mary, Queen of Scots' House,
Queen Street, Jedburgh, Scotland.
This house tells the tragic story of the life of
Mary Stuart.

Parham House,
Parham Park, Pulborough,
West Sussex, RH20 4HS
Tel: 0903 742021
This beautiful Elizabethan house has a good
collection of Tudor furniture, portraits and
needlework.

The Elizabethan House,
32 New Street, Plymouth
Tel: 0752 668000
This Elizabethan house contains furniture
from the Tudor and Stuart periods.

The Shakespeare Birthplace Trust owns five
Tudor houses and the Shakespeare
Countryside Museum. To arrange a guided
bus tour, telephone 0789 294466.

MUSEUMS

Mary Rose Ship Hall and Exhibition,
H.M. Naval Base, College Road,
Portsmouth PO1 3LX
Tel: 0705 750521
The exhibition features many of the
thousands of objects recovered during the
excavations of the Mary Rose, Henry VIII's
favourite warship.

The Museum of London,
London Wall, London, EC2Y 5HN
Tel: 071 600 3699
This museum has a good collection of Tudor
artefacts.

The Shakespeare Globe Museum and The
Rose Theatre Exhibition,
Bear Gardens, London SE1
Tel: 071 928 6342
It houses a permanent exhibition covering
the history of London theatre from
1576-1642.

Totnes Museum,
70 Fore Street, Totnes, South Devon, TQ9 5RU
Tel: 0803 863821
The museum has a small collection of Tudor
pottery, panelling and furniture housed in a
four-storey Elizabethan merchant's house.

Tudor House Museum,
St. Michael's Square, Bugle Street,
Southampton, Hampshire
Tel: 0703 332513
Behind this late 15th/early 16th century
timber-framed house there is an accurate
reconstruction of a 16th century garden.

INDEX

Additional photographs: AA Picture Library 13; Bodleian Library, University of Oxford 26; Bridgeman Art Library 6(1) and cover/Belvoir Castle, Leicestershire, 8(r)/The Bible Society, London, 29(t)/Institute of Directors, London, 29(b)/The British Library, London; The College of Arms 25 (The Westminster Tournament Roll); A.F. Kersting 7(1), 18, 23(t); National Maritime Museum 12; National Portrait Gallery 5, 6(r), 11(both); Royal Collection, St. James's Palace © HM The Queen 10(r); Richard Sorrell 7(r).